Marketing management for beginners

How to create and establish your brand with the right marketing management, build sustainable customer relationships and increase sales despite a buyer's market

Sebastian Wahlig

CONTENT

What can you expect in this book?

Are you interested in marketing management, but need a summary of the basics to properly understand it and evaluate opportunities for yourself? Then this guide is just what you need: Intelligent marketing management is an important tool for brand building and sustainable customer loyalty.

Here you will get an introduction to marketing management and its most important basic principles: What does the term actually mean these days and what goals does it pursue?

Surely you have heard of the well-known marketing mix, but what exactly is behind it? What about the existing market, how are demarcations made and how do you develop a suitable marketing strategy on the basis of this information in order to be able to retain customers in the long term?

You will get easy-to-understand answers to all these questions in this book, which will help you get an overall view of the basics.

You'll also get important practice tips and a 10-step action plan for building your own marketing plan.

Introduction

In German, the term marketing means sales management and encompasses a wide range of strategies and corporate activities with the aim of presenting and ultimately selling a brand, product or service to one or more target groups. In the process, marketing management has undergone a major transformation over the past 100 years: The marketing we know today did not emerge until the end of the 19th century, because until then there were still the old familiar seller's markets. The range of products on offer was still very small compared to today, which is why the number of potential customers was concentrated on fewer products from which a selection had to be made. With the advance of industrialization and the resulting mass production, the number of products grew and the so-called buyer's markets emerged: a continuously growing number of suppliers compete for a smaller number of customers who are eligible for the product.

> **Good to know!** In today's buyer's market, it's no longer about a customer buying a product at all, but the motto is: "Buy my products instead of my competitor's."

TARGETS

Why should you learn about and use marketing activities? Quite simply, as you have already learned in the above paragraph, markets today are structured very differently and competition is very high in most industries. So you need to reach your potential customers somehow to convince them about your product or service.

But here, too, you need to distinguish and define what exactly your business goal is before you can start developing a marketing strategy. Do you primarily want to promote your brand or go straight into selling specific products?

Here is an overview of the key branding objectives:

• Generate the image of a brand (to be built)

• Increase the reach and awareness

• Retain customers through satisfaction and thus create brand loyalty

• Increase buyer penetration (i.e..: How large is the share of buyers of a brand in relation to the total of all buyers of a specific product group?).

• Increase purchase volume

• Communicate brand competence

In contrast, the primary goals in sales marketing are as follows:

• Bring about more sales

• Increase sales and contribution margin

• Increase profitability

• Increase market share

• Expand profit

• Raise price level

• Expand distribution level.

MARKETING MIX

Today's market offers countless providers of products and services around the world.

All these producers are in competition with each other and therefore need to differentiate their products from those of others.

In this context, the so-called marketing mix shows various ways of making such a differentiation. The brand ting mix consists of the classic "four P's", which summarize all marketing areas that contribute to achieving the objectives.

- Product (product policy)
- Price (pricing policy)
- Place (distribution policy)
- Promotion (communication policy).

It is particularly important here that all areas or activities are precisely coordinated with one another. You could also say that the marketing mix translates abstract strategies into concrete plans. In the following, we will take a closer look at the individual instruments:

Product - product policy

The most important part of a company is the products or services that are to be sold.

Thus, this pillar includes all activities associated with this product. The product policy is therefore of significant importance in the marketing mix, because it is the central element of every company. At the same time, it forms the basis for the other marketing measures. In this context, it is crucial to determine the product life cycle and to take it into account during planning.

The following issues can be discussed in product policy:

- Which products are to be distributed on the market?
- What does the packaging look like?
- Is it necessary to take an existing product off the market?

Price - pricing policy

When planning marketing, price plays an important role, which, incidentally, has been the case since well before the concept of marketing came into being. Here, then, it is a matter of considering how the company wishes to build up its pricing in order to achieve a fair price-performance ratio and, at the same time, to generate as high a profit as possible. Covered are questions such as:

- What price should my product get?
- Should there possibly be discounts?
- What are the shipping and delivery options?

Place - Distribution policy
Distribution policy is concerned with measures that address the distribution of the product or service offered. Among other things, the following must be clarified:

- Where should the product be sold?
- At what point or in what time frame?
- Are wholesalers and retailers interposed or is the product distributed directly to the customer?
- Are there target quantities when selling this product?

Promotion - communication policy
This refers to all the means used to sell the products and address the customers.

Elementary questions include:

- How and where should the product be advertised?
- For example, is it to be exhibited at a trade fair or advertised on television?
- What can a social media presence look like?

Now that all areas have been addressed, we would like to clarify why a good marketing mix is so important. The sensible bundling of all planned measures ensures that a defined target group can be effectively addressed and, ideally, sustainably tied to the company.

In this context, the effectiveness of the activities carried out depends heavily on preceding objectives, which is why a large investment of thought and strategy pays off in advance. Since the marketing mix is aimed at addressing customers, it therefore directly affects a company's sales and profits.

Markets and market participants

INTRODUCTION TO MARKET RESEARCH

Marketing decisions require a wide range of information about the market. This involves, for example, knowledge about customers, the competition and, of course, the company's own business situation.

The task of market research is therefore the comprehensive determination of this information or, in scientific terms, the systematic exploration of a defined submarket. It is significant for every company in order to establish itself successfully on the market. Market research is a subfield of marketing research with the essential difference that the latter focuses predominantly on the situation in the company and is thus not limited to the markets.

Market research tasks include:

• The identification of comprehensive information about the crucial sales markets

• Assistance in selecting the most suitable marketing measures (evaluation function)

• Contribution to the continuous optimization of various measures and identification of the causes of possible failures (control function)

• The recognition of trends and developments (innovation function)

• The determination of risks (early warning function)

• Support for decision-making (uncertainty reduction function)

• Increasing the level of internal decision-making.

Types of market research
Depending on what is to be studied, a distinction is made between demoscopic and ecoscopic market research:

Demoscopic market research is responsible for subject-related data collection on individual market participants, such as age, gender, marital status, income or occupation, while **ecoscopic market research** explores object-related industry data such as sales, product qualities or prices. The basis for the latter is the nature of the markets and includes factors such as the number of existing buyers and suppliers.

A further distinction in the field of market research is made between primary and secondary research. While in **primary research** (field research), data is obtained from direct contact with market participants, **secondary research** works with existing findings (desk research). We will briefly discuss both types:

Primary research

This is an empirical method of initial data collection that can be conducted on a one-time or recurring basis. Since it is very costly, it is usually implemented by large corporations or institutions and uses both qualitative and quantitative methods.

Qualitative methods can be interviews, workshops, or observations and typically rely on a small group of people who, while not representative of the whole, offer deeper insight into their decision-making.

In contrast, quantitative primary research involves larger groups of several thousand people who provide their information, e.g., with the help of standardized questionnaires, thus creating the basis for a statistical analysis.

As examples, the following methods can be mentioned:

- Survey (written, telephone, personal, online)
- Observation (field, laboratory)
- Experiment (field, laboratory, store)
- Consumer panel (documentation of purchasing behavior, especially in the area of consumer goods).

Secondary research

As mentioned at the beginning, secondary research works with already existing data and derives findings from it. The processing and interpretation of this external data can come from the following sources:

• Databases

• Annual Reports

• Official statistics

• Books and journals

• Price lists

• Address books

• Internet

• Studies

• Marketing materials of the competition (e.g. catalogs)

• Association news

• Patent publications.

The goals of secondary research can be of different nature. For example, it may reveal that there is a need for primary research to clarify a particular issue, or the data obtained may be used to make assumptions and explain problems in more detail.

However, it is always of central importance that the relevance of the primary data in relation to the research question is assured and that the data are up-to-date, complete, credible and free from subjective influence.

Advantages and disadvantages of primary and secondary research

Primary research	Secondary research
Advantages:	*Advantages:*
• authentic data	• Information is relatively easy and quick to obtain
• current	
• exclusive	• cheaper
• data obtained are related to a specific question, accurate and relevant to the decision to be made.	• partly only one data source
	• to find many possible fields of information online.

Disadvantages:	*Disadvantages:*
• time and cost intensive	• Limited availability
• high personnel expenditure	• partly unspecific or too general
• good, own knowledge required	• limited topicality
• often only feasible with external help due to the high effort involved.	• inappropriate level of detail
	• not exclusive, because generally accessible
	• little comparable for different sources.

> **Good to know**: Information from secondary research should always be checked and used first, because it is considered basic data and makes it easier to get started with the problem. They also contribute to the cost-effectiveness of market research.

So, as you have seen above, there are many aspects to consider with both research methods . But why is market research so important? The following two examples illustrate what can happen if the situation on the sales markets is ignored and trends are simply not noticed:

For a long time, the world-famous computer company IBM focused exclusively on the production and sale of mainframes and realized the market development towards PCs and laptops much too late. This was a serious mistake that meant huge missed profit opportunities for the company and could have been avoided with appropriate market research.

A second example is the American auto industry, which for several decades produced only for the domestic market and, due to the favorable price of gasoline, also produced almost exclusively large passenger cars with correspondingly high gasoline consumption.

This had the disadvantage that these models were poorly suited for export, which then became the car industry's undoing when gasoline prices in the U.S. rose significantly and smaller, more fuel-efficient models from Japan sold better. The American auto industry thus had to involuntarily give up important market shares - resulting in a crisis that has left its mark to this day.

These two examples clearly show that it is vital for every company to constantly monitor and analyze market developments and to act sustainably on the basis of the findings.

From an economic point of view, a market is the meeting of supply and demand or the transfer of rights of disposal. But what is meant by the definition of a market? A market definition is intended to determine the relevant market of a company and, in this context, to determine whether it holds a dominant position or even a monopoly. These tasks are usually performed by the antitrust authorities, who delineate the market under consideration in terms of **product**, **geography** and **time.**

The banana producer Chiquita can be taken as an example of the importance of market definitions: If it is assumed that the company sells "fruit," the corresponding calculation results in a market share of only about 5 percent. However, if pure banana production is assumed, this share rises to around 50 percent, indicating high market power. In such a case, close monitoring must take place so that, if necessary, direct intervention can be taken. In practice, however, it is more likely that the entire fruit market would be delineated in this case, since it can be assumed that a sharp price increase would divert customer demand for bananas to other types of fruit. The fulfillment of certain characteristics of a product thus also plays an important role.

The different types of market definition are briefly explained below:

Factual market definition

The factual market definition is the heart of the market determination and brings to light which products and services the relevant market offers at the present time. This is also referred to as the demand market concept. The supply market under consideration includes all products and services that are substitutable with respect to the consumer's needs in terms of function, characteristics and price. However, the habits of customers should not be underestimated here: Dry and wet razors, for example, are substitutable for each other, but once a customer has become accustomed to a certain type of shave and is satisfied with it, a change is rather unlikely.

However, producers also play a major role in the topic of market delineation and possible market dominance. A producer can always adapt its offered products and services according to the needs of the customers. However, further information is often needed to make a factual market delineation, which is why various tests have been introduced. For example, an SSNIP test can check the consequences of a small price increase on purchasing behavior, which is carried out over a longer period of time. This then determines whether the clientele would possibly switch to another, similar product.

Spatial market definition

Both interchangeability in terms of function and criteria in production play a role here. A good example of the former is the production of vacuum cleaner bags for the best-known brand products. Here, retailers are able to cover the existing demand with producers from different European countries (functional criterion). For production-related characteristics, the example of car drivers who wish to register their vehicle with the relevant road traffic office can be used. These are usually dependent on the sign embossing companies located in the immediate vicinity.

Market definition in terms of time

As a final, somewhat subordinate distinction for market definition, there is the temporal variant. Thus, a Christmas market held in December may be a relevant market where the competitive situation will not change because the largest number of firms will only be active in that time frame. Consequently, there is no need to divide the competitive situation into different time periods.

Market definition vs. market segmentation
Segmenting a market means first capturing it and then dividing it up.

Market segmentation divides the overall market and examines further factors with adequate marketing instruments. Possible segmentations are, for example, products or customers, whereby further distinctions can be made within these criteria (in the case of customers, for example, according to age, gender or profession). In the case of product segmentation, for example, a categorization can be carried out with the aid of annual financial statement data. The creation of competitive advantages and the avoidance of substitution effects are among the most important objectives in market segmentation. In the segmentation process, the company can once again identify itself precisely and create a demarcation from the overall market to be considered. Furthermore, submarkets should be determined here and possible market gaps uncovered.

Marketing develop strategies and plans

ANALYSIS OF THE INITIAL SITUATION

Before planning and creating a marketing strategy, a detailed analysis of the current initial situation should be carried out. The most important goals here are the determination of conditions and changes, but also the recognition of opportunities and risks. For a company that wants to operate successfully in the market, it is essential to be well informed about the current market conditions as well as the overall economic situation.

The timely perception of changes is equally

crucial in order to be able to react quickly and exploit emerging opportunities and circumvent risks.

The strategic baseline is usually undertaken in the following two broad areas:

• Analysis of the environment (market situation, customer needs)

• Analysis of the company situation.

Environment

The analysis of global factors, i.e. the macro-environment, includes the analysis of current as well as future developments in the areas of overall economy, politics, society, technology and law.

The ever-increasing use of smartphones, for example, is a trend that is of particular importance for many sectors and should be monitored closely. Technological and social developments can, after all, be of great importance to many companies, as many opportunities arise here. However, this requires the company to keep a watchful eye on the market so that no competitive disadvantages arise.

For example, the large electronics manufacturer Siemens missed out on the development of cameras, color and touch displays at the time, and was henceforth unable to compete in this market and had to sell it.

Market situation

As the technical term suggests, the analysis of the market situation is much more specific to the relevant market. The basic characteristics of this market, such as market growth, are essential in this context. But also possible changes in the needs of the customers and their behavior are significant, because all customers of the relevant market are examined, not only already existing ones. Finally, it is important to mention the competitors, because it is crucial to know who exactly they are and what their goals and strategies are.

A popular tool for market analysis is Porter's industry structure analysis, which analyzes the attractiveness of an industry using 5 competitive forces and provides information about the structural characteristics of a particular industry.

Competitor analysis is also important. Here, the strengths and weaknesses of both direct and indirect competitors compared to one's own company are determined. The aim is to define competitive advantages.

Further analysis options of the activity sector are the assessment of the market size, its growth opportunities and the current phase in the industry life cycle. The wider environment can be looked at in more detail using a so-called STEP analysis. The STEP analysis describes the current developments in the macroeconomic environment by means of 4 dimensions:

- Socio-cultural influences
- Economic influences
- Technological influences
- Political-regulatory influences.

Customer needs

In addition to developments in the wider environment and the structure of the industry, it is very important to focus on trends in the industry itself. Market requirements must be identified and customer needs discussed. Without customers, a company cannot continue to exist, which is why it is essential to focus on the demand side and build one's company in a "client centric" way.

With a so-called model of life phases, initial customer areas with the same or similar needs can be derived and examined. This represents an essential step on the way to understanding customer expectations and wishes and helps to be able to act "client centric".

Therefore, Customer Centricity is also of great importance for the strategy of the company. In the further strategy process, understanding the needs of customers can also be very important, for example if it makes sense to make the organizational structure even more customer-oriented as part of the strategy implementation.

Life stages model
Childhood→ Education→ Starting a career → Starting a family→ Establishing oneself in the profession→ Consolidating in the profession→ Retirement age→ Passing away

A suitable means of consolidating the most important findings from the analysis of the environment is the opportunity/threat profile. In the further course, these can then be assessed in greater depth, for example in a SWOT analysis, together with the findings from the business analysis.

A future picture is an excellent way of summarizing the key market trends. It shows where the sales market is likely to move over a defined time horizon (e.g., 3 or 8 years). It includes key statements from the respective development areas (e.g., health or digitization) and provides a concise and plausible summary of the analysis phase. This picture of the future now sets the framework for the subsequent strategy process.

Use case: Preparation of a picture of the future with trends for the Swiss healthcare market

A large insurance company set itself the task of developing a strategy process. As part of the analysis of the initial situation, a picture of the future was created. There were already some fragments from the environment analysis, which came from internal as well as external sources.

The first task was to compile these. The following factors played a role in our example for the healthcare market in Switzerland:

- personalized medicine
- increasing specialization
- Customer needs
- Digitization
- increased regulation.

In the second step, the missing components were now to be found and supplemented, for which a workshop was initiated. Here, the elements of the future vision were discussed and adapted by the strategy team.

With the picture of the future now complete, all participants agreed on which trends and market changes would be important for the insurance company. For all subsequent steps in strategy development, it is now essential to focus on the most important developments, since the future picture already provides detailed documentation of developments in the corporate environment.

Finally, 10 strategic prerequisites were derived from the picture of the future, which in turn showed what action the company would need to take in the coming years. Furthermore, assumptions about the future business model were presented:

Sales market: The healthcare market is being strongly influenced by consolidation in the inpatient sector and by new offerings and business ideas in the outpatient sector.

Customer needs: The requirements and wishes of customers differ according to their stage of life, group affiliation and other factors.

Environment: Increasing environmental awareness is making sustainable and environmentally friendly product solutions more and more popular in virtually all industries.

Company situation

This internal analysis of the company takes place in the second step of the initial analysis. In contrast to the environment analysis, the internal characteristics of the company are to be closely examined and assessed here. The aim is to identify strengths and weaknesses. The application of various methods, such as the consideration of product life cycles, the SWOT analysis or benchmarking is also essential here for a realistic assessment.

Analysis of competencies and resources

An assessment of competencies or business capabilities reveals where the respective strengths and weaknesses are to be found. It is always function-related and should show precisely those capabilities that are of central importance for the respective business model.

Resource analysis, on the other hand, is not function-based and is based on the following 4 characteristics:

- Non-imitability
- Non-substitutability
- Company specificity
- Ability to produce customer value.

Here, it is particularly important to define the so-called core competencies, as strategically relevant competencies and resources play a central role for a company. Core competencies create the following foundations:

- They contribute significantly to customer benefit.
- They are individual and difficult to imitate.
- They can be transferred to new sales markets and products.

Analysis of own competitiveness
Now remember back to the analysis of the environment. Here, the market situation has already been analyzed with the competitive environment. Now - as part of the company analysis - it is time to take a close look at your own competitiveness by comparing your own strengths and weaknesses with those of the competitor companies . The following questions can help here:

- Does my organization have strengths that can be

barriers to entry or weaknesses that reduce the effectiveness of those barriers?

• Which strengths and weaknesses influence my negotiating position with customers and suppliers?

• What are the strengths and weaknesses of my company's size compared to the competition?

Analysis of the product life cycle

There are two ways in which the product life cycle can be viewed for strategic business analysis:

• Product and program policy

• Demands on the functional areas.

Product life cycle analysis is used to determine and discuss the optimal assortment composition and structure.

The individual phases in the product life cycle require different compositions in the functional areas. This concept thus provides us with various points of reference for the phase-specific issues surrounding the introduction, growth, maturity, saturation and possible further development of a product.

Analysis of the company structure

The review of the corporate structure is also an essential point. Depending on which strategy(s) are determined in the subsequent strategy process, modifications to the organizational structure may become important. Therefore, the advantages and disadvantages as well as pain points of the current structure must already be considered in the analysis phase.

Analysis of the company culture
This analysis reveals the essential values underlying the behavior of the company as well as its employees and answers questions that will be essential later in the strategy process (e.g., whether a strategic option can be compatible with the organizational culture).

All findings from the company analysis are included in a so-called strengths/weaknesses profile and should therefore be looked at in greater depth as part of a SWOT analysis together with the results from the analysis of the environment.

The company analysis and the results of the environment analysis now form a basis for further strategy considerations.

SELECTION OF SUITABLE STRATEGIES

Based on the analysis of the initial situation, it is now possible to answer the following key questions:

> - **What?** I.e.: Which strategy goals are being pursued?
> - **With whom?** Who is/are my target group(s)?
> - **Until when?**

In detail, these questions can then be formulated as follows:

• What are the priorities with regard to the various market areas? Especially if you have a large budget, it makes sense to look carefully at which subareas you want to focus on.

• What proportion of existing marketing resources should be allocated to existing customers and what proportion to new customers?

• What goals are to be achieved by when? Criteria such as the corporate image, customer satisfaction or the services offered play a role here.

• What timing for achieving market success-related goals should be targeted (e.g., customer count or average purchase frequency)?

• Which economic marketing goals are important to us and should be realized (sales and profit)?

These basic strategic questions about the company's positioning in the competitive environment and about customer benefits can be asked as part of the strategy selection process:

• What benefit can our company offer to the customer? A distinction must be made here between the basic benefit and the additional benefit: The basic benefit includes the central performance aspect that is expected, e.g. the transport function of a car. The additional benefit is supplementary and particularly important in the area of similar competitive products. Here, attempts are often made to create an additional psychological benefit by means of advertising and to make the product appear desirable, e.g., the particularly good appearance of the car or the expected gain in prestige.

Other types of benefits include economic benefits (low price, helpful in saving money), process-related benefits (easy to acquire and use, easy to understand, simple handling, no waiting time, etc.), emotional/social benefits (trends, promising, industry knowledge, etc.).

• What advantages over the competition does our organization strive to achieve?
This question is essential for the pursuit of a competitive strategy.
This is a part of the marketing strategy and deals with the strategic, customer-related behavior in the sales

market. The most commonly pursued competitive strategies are cost leadership (i.e., the lowest prices in the sector), differentiation (e.g., very good customer relations, better products, etc.), and niche strategy (specializing in a niche where there is no competition). In short, the organization stands out through a special performance) and the niche strategy (specialization in a niche in which there is only a relatively small number of customers, but which is often quite demanding, this is the route taken by the sports car manufacturer Porsche, for example).

Strategy issues for innovation orientation
What level of innovation orientation do we want to achieve in our organization? There are the following strategy types for this purpose:

• **Defender:** Innovation orientation is low, this often occurs with niche strategies.

• **Analyzer:** The innovation orientation is medium and the willingness to take risks is not particularly high. On the other hand, opportunities for success are carefully analyzed.

• **Prospector:** The focus on innovation is high. There is an ongoing and active search for new opportunities. The associated willingness to take risks is high.

To what extent should focal points be set for new product development and the opening up of new markets? There are 4 strategy types for this:

• **Market penetration:** The degree of innovation is low. The organization focuses on existing products in developed markets. Nevertheless, the opportunity for innovation still exists.

• **Product development:** New development, revision or further development of products offered in existing markets. The supplementation of products with services (additional benefits) is also to be regarded as part of this. This means that the current range of services can be expanded (product range expansion) or even replaced (product substitution).

• **Market development: Existing** products are to be marketed in a new sales market. This may involve geographical areas, other distribution channels or new target groups.

• **Diversification: The** degree of innovation is highest here, i.e., newly developed products are offered in markets that have not been addressed before.

Strategy issues for the management of customer relationships

How can the company ensure the loyalty of its customers? It is necessary to distinguish:

• **Contractual ties:** The customer is bound to the company by a contract. This often takes place for a fixed period of time or on the basis of quantity specifications.

• **Technical-functional link:** A specific product can only be used with another product from the company in question (e.g. Nespresso can only be made with the coffee machine designed for it).

• **Psychological attachment:** This includes factors such as customer satisfaction, certain habits or loyalty to a brand (e.g. the family has always driven VW). The psychological bond of a customer can be strengthened or promoted by the following measures: good and fast customer service, accommodating handling of complaints, individual special offers, bonus programs, volume and loyalty discounts, etc.

• **Economic commitment:** This can be, for example, a reward offered to the customer or the fact that switching would be uneconomical for the demander. A good example here is the monthly flat rate in fitness studios.

How can the purchase of large quantities be supported or the purchase of small quantities be avoided? One possibility is to use low-quantity surcharges, i.e. for small orders, the surcharge should be set in such a way that it covers the material costs and also ensures a minimum profit.

Strategy issues on competitive and collaborative behavior:

• **Threatening competitive behavior: In** pricing policy, for example, this includes a com promiseless, heavily advertised low-price policy. In communications policy, high spending on advertising leads to a large reach and thus a large number of customers. This represents a high barrier to market entry. In distribution policy, strong control of sales channels counts as threatening competitive behavior. In product policy, a large product portfolio means a higher cost for imitators. Last but not least, the management of customer relations should now be addressed: Here, deterrence for competitors can be achieved by the existence of a very high level of loyalty.

• **Cooperative behavior:** For example, a company can work with a competitor to create certain market entry gaps for further competitors. Another possibility is to create mutual access to know-how and further resources (experience reports, advertising options, relationships).

• Sales synergies are also part of cooperative behavior, which includes, for example, brokerage with commission or so-called cross-selling (German:

Querververkauf, i.e. exploiting an existing customer relationship for the sale of complementary products or services). These types of cooperation with competitor companies can be very advantageous, especially if the budget is small.

Strategy questions on the basic structure of the marketing mix:
• To what extent should individual customer segments be differentiated in processing?

• Should customer processing be standardized or segment-specific?

• Which price positioning (low price, medium price, high price position) should be adopted? Companies wishing to enter a new market often temporarily aim for an exceptionally favorable price-performance ratio.

• How high should the marketing budget be set and what distribution should be made among the individual marketing instruments?

To summarize the strategy considerations, the selected strategy should always meet the following 4 criteria:

• It is essential that the marketing strategy has compatibility with the corporate strategy and that there are no contradictions arising from measures and objectives.

• The strategy needs sufficient information as a basis.

• The content meaning of the marketing strategy must be accurate and appropriate.

• The feasibility of implementation must be realistic in terms of available resources and conceivable counter-reactions from the competition.

Example from practice

The following example shows how the development of a holistic, successful marketing strategy could look in practice:

A recently founded company sells outdoor and leisure clothing according to its own design. Sales are made both in retail stores in a small town and via the company's online store. The creation of a marketing strategy could now look as follows:

SWOT analysis of the initial situation

• There are no stores nearby that have similar products in their assortment (= opportunity).

• There is a lot of competition (= risk) in online trading.

• An individual plus point is the own design (= strength).

- There is no clientele yet (= weakness).

Objective

- A customer base must be built up in both brick-and-mortar and online retail (customer numbers should be defined as target values).

- The brand must be established.

- Sales for the first fiscal year must be planned.

Decision making for the different measures

- A corporate design must be developed (definition of corporate colors, development of a logo, definition of imagery, etc.).

- There is to be a coupon promotion for the new opening (both online and via flyers distributed regionally).

- A sports event is to be sponsored in the city.

- A blog around the topic of outdoor activities is to be launched. The texts used should be prepared SEO-compliant and there should be a link to the newsletter registration in the context of e-mail marketing.

- A community is to be built on social media platforms (Facebook, Instagram, etc.).

- Affiliate cooperations in the outdoor sector are being planned.

Success measurement

- The development of the number of customers must

be continuously monitored, also in relation to the individual marketing strategies.

• Both revenue channels require constant monitoring (online and offline).

• In the context of cost control, it should be discussed which marketing strategies are profitable and which are not.

TIPS FOR AN EFFECTIVE MARKETING STRATEGY

Of course, choosing wisely and linking multiple sub-strategies are important to the success of marketing in the enterprise. However, there are other aspects that also play into it. So pay special attention to these points:

Always keep your target group in mind
Think about which marketing strategy will best reach your customers. For example, a heterogeneous clientele in a highly competitive market can best be addressed using guerrilla or event marketing. The various online marketing measures, on the other hand, are better suited to target groups that are very devoted to the Internet and online shopping.

Think about your success measurement
You can only measure the success of a marketing strategy by repeatedly monitoring its success. Only then will it become apparent whether the measures applied have paid off or whether it would be better to invest in other methods. One advantage of online marketing is that the measurement of success can be supported here by appropriate tools.

Combine online and offline strategies

A good complement of marketing strategies from the online and offline areas can pay off. If an open day is taking place, for example, this should be shared on social media. This is how you combine event marketing with social media marketing.

Use a CRM system

CRM stands for Customer Relationship Management and is a software for managing and mapping customer management. It helps companies maintain an overview of their customer relationships and paves the way for improved service and individualized marketing strategies.

Include existing resources

Every marketing strategy has different costs. Therefore, when planning, consider what resources are already available and how they can be used efficiently and profitably.

Review your strategy regularly and adjust it if necessary

Companies and sales markets are subject to constant development. Therefore, it is important to regularly review the applied marketing strategy and make necessary adjustments.

Important! A marketing strategy will only appeal to your clientele if it can offer added value. This can be different things, such as information, entertainment or a community feeling.

Create customer loyalty

BASICS OF BRAND BUILDING

Challenging and exciting at the same time - this is probably the best way to describe the topic of brand building in the context of brand management. The challenge is not a small one, but with a well-considered basic structure, optimal processes, the availability of required resources, and consideration of proven procedures and success factors, successful brand building can be achieved by companies of any size.

What is meant by brand building?
Building a brand consists of planning, organizing, implementing and controlling all the relevant measures of a company with the aim of creating a clearly

differentiated emotional image of the customer associated with a company or product.

Brand building is not the same as advertising or sales. There is much more to building a brand than advertising or distributing it. Regarding the latter, it should even be mentioned that many brands have already been destroyed by sales staff or sales executives, because too many discounts or price reductions mean death for a long-established and proven brand. Of course, a brand also needs media, multipliers and structured customer communication, but especially in B2B, advertising is far from being everything.

Vision, commitment, implementation - three central characteristics of brand building. It takes a clear vision to develop a brand. Only then can employees be carried along and the appropriate tools be used. For this reason, it is also essential to anchor brand thinking in the management, because that is precisely where visions and strategies are born. Next, the employees must be addressed in order to support this brand vision and to be able to build up a commitment as a whole. In the third step, suitable communication and sales channels can be selected to further build up and establish the brand.

Why is brand building so important?
Brands have a fundamental advantage, both for their owners and for companies: As a **communication tool,** they are important for the efficient operation of a company, both for internal and external marketing.

Brands are a **driver of profitability**: Various scientific studies show that the brand value (reputation) achieved through mass communication has a particularly positive impact on the profitability of the companies studied.

In conclusion, it can be said that the value of a company can be increased with the help of a brand.

But brands also create **identity**. They are adapted and have an identity-forming function for customers or social groups. With the help of the brand, customers can differentiate themselves or demonstrate a sense of belonging by using the brand. This is a social function that can be achieved by emotionalizing a brand.

Brands contribute to identification. In highly competitive markets, where people are often overwhelmed by the variety of products on offer, they can act as a beacon and provide orientation. The brand offers a recognition value, creates trust and thus facilitates the purchase decision for the customer. This principle applies to both business marketing (B2B) and consumer marketing (B2C).

Brands promise quality. A brand always contains a verbal or non-verbal statement about the quality of the product. For this reason, it is enormously important to discuss the company's understanding of quality before building the brand. What promises do we want to make with our brand? Which customer expectations should be fulfilled with our products and services and which should not?

Brands are innovation bases. It is much easier for strong and established brands to introduce innovations to the market. Existing brands have the advantage of the benefit of trust and the existing innovation landscape. As a result, product innovations can be introduced with significantly less effort and encounter a prepared market situation.

Brands anchor customer loyalty

Brands offer opportunities to bind customers to a company in the long term. Customers who have once found their way to a brand and stay for satisfaction are profitable for the organization and secure the business model. This increases customer value and, in the long term, the value of the company. Although large investments are sometimes necessary at the beginning when building a brand, these pay off if the brand is managed correctly, so that the returns from the brand far exceed the original investment.

Brands mean bargaining power

In negotiations, strong brands can score with competitive advantages and provide additional revenue.

When is the right time to start looking at building a brand?

A brand is not built on the side. The fact that it requires a well thought-out concept and sensible implementation has already been explained in detail. However, there are three different starting points for determining when the time is right:

Start-ups: Of course, it stands to reason that as a start-up you have to think about how you want to build your brands. But is that really the case? Especially in the start-up phase, the variety of tasks involved, the general uncertainty at the beginning, the sales situation and the financial pressure can be overwhelming. Often, questions about brand management are pushed into the background for the time being. Nevertheless, important questions should be clarified, especially in this delicate initial phase:

- What should our brand stand for?
- What performance and benefits do we promise?

- Which target group is interesting?

- What is our recognition value?

It is advisable to get outside support for this. Even if the financial scope in the start-up phase is limited, a brand consultant can provide a lot of good assistance in this process and thus shorten the learning curve.

Product launch

In product management, there is often a desire to make a product stand out and to specify it in the overall context of the company. In this context, it makes particular sense to think about the profiling of a brand whenever product innovations are introduced that are on the edge of the performance curve. In the digital transformation era, many companies are changing direction and venturing into new business areas and sales markets. Where appropriate, brand building can then provide access to potential new customers, additional contacts or new business areas. The decision to launch just one new product or an entire brand is not an easy one. Considered alternatives should be explored with external help, since often only an external professional partner has the necessary distance to be able to rationally assess such an elementary decision.

From product manufacturer to brand company

Especially in the B2B sector, a development from a pure product manufacturer to a sales-oriented company and later to a brand company often takes place after some time. Especially in times of digitalization, many companies have to think about differentiation from the competition and move away from a pure consideration of products.

The transformation to a brand company can thus be a differentiator and open up new opportunities. It is then not just manufacturing and the resulting product that is the focus, but the interest of the customers. Consider taking a customer perspective as a solution approach. This combined with positioning yourself as an expert in the relevant area offers great growth opportunities and better revenue opportunities than focusing purely on the product. B2B companies should seek outside support in this transformation to learn to see boundaries in practice and new ways of thinking.

WHAT ARE THE MOST IM-PORTANT STEPS IN BUILDING BRANDS?

To make sure that the branding gets structure, the following approach should be applied:

Analysis of the current brand positioning
A fundamental step in the brand building process is an evaluation and analysis of the given market position-ing. There is always an existing feeling or perception in the company and among employees about the posi-tion of the brand.

However, this self-perception can differ from the external perception of a company, because areas such as administration, sales, marketing and production of-ten have very different views of the position of the Un terprise and its own brand. Unfortunately, there are no well-founded studies or reports on external perception in practice. Many companies from the B2B sector lack a reliable customer centricity approach and thus infor-mation about current market positioning.

Analysis of the sales market and the competitive situation
What market are we actually operating in? Who is my competition? What approach will customers take with

products and solutions in the future? Since the external view is a challenging circumstance, especially in an international context, it is worthwhile to involve an external partner or a consulting firm so that an objective view is guaranteed. Above all, questions about the relevant competitive position and customer requirements should be addressed with a market analysis. Of course, the results of the market analysis carried out as part of the development of a marketing strategy can also be used here - provided that they are close in time.

Analysis of customer structures
The precise identification of potential customer structures is an equally significant step in brand building. It is in the power of a brand to reach out to the relevant target group, generate interaction there, and ultimately drive sales with them. Within this customer base, brands help to identify a profile, differentiate and find their position with customers.

Of course, not every brand is made for everyone. It therefore makes sense to use customer insights to get closer to the customers and see what their wishes and requirements are in relation to the product area and the brand environment. Without these customer insights, efficient brand development is basically impossible.

Building the brand positioning

Based on the market and customer structure analysis, it is now time to develop the brand positioning. This should state how the company or the brand should act in the environment of customers, competition and various performance requirements at present and in the future. The positioning of the brand should generate added value for the company and its customers.

Legal framework

In the sensible and flawless construction of a brand, care should also be taken to ensure that it is optimally protected legally. There are different approaches: A trademark can be protected as a word mark or as a word-picture mark.

Word mark protection is the greatest possible because it protects any spelling, font, font size, upper or lower case. However, it is often unfortunately not possible to obtain word mark protection. This is especially the case if the brand name contains colloquial words that are not registrable.

A word-picture mark, on the other hand, is related to a specific graphic design. This means that when assessing the likelihood of confusion with other trademarks, not only the word element is taken into account, but also the graphic elements used.

Consequently, it can happen that an already existing trademark is infringed because the same fonts or similar graphics are used. A trademark is generally registered at the Trademark and Patent Office in Munich. If the trademark is to be protected throughout Europe, it is registered at the European Trademark and Patent Office in Alicante, Spain.

THE SUPPLY AND DEMAND CURVE

In order to be able to build up a market supply, some basics about supply and demand knowledge are needed. Here we will look at the supply and demand curve and learn what the mathematical relationship is between supply, demand and price.

Supply curve

The supply describes the quantity of a good offered for sale by different sellers on the market. The law of supply states: If the price increases, then the quantity offered increases accordingly and vice versa.

The positive relationship between quantity and price is converted from the supply function into a mathematical formula. The supply curve then shows the mathematical relationship graphically in a price-quantity diagram, from which it can be read what price a product has for a given supply quantity.

> **Important. The** sum of all offered quantities on a sales market is called aggregate market supply.

A good example is the fish market. Assume that there are only 2 stalls, each of which sells 4 fish. If external influences change this market situation, e.g. due to decreasing fish stocks, the supply changes independently of the supply price. This increases or decreases the supply and causes a shift of the aggregate curve to the right or to the left.

In combination with the demand function, the market equilibrium is determined.

In principle, one first assumes that the price alone determines the supply quantity. However, it is also possible that the supply is reduced or increased by a development of the market situation. But what exactly causes this change in the supply quantity if not the price? So it must be external factors that change this market situation. There are 5 factors that can shift the supply curve. Here, an increase in supply leads to a shift to the right, while a decrease leads to a shift to the left.

The price of relevant **production factors** also plays a major role. If, for example, the price of fishing nets increases in purchasing, less is offered (left shift).

If, on the other hand, the price of crude oil falls, less money is needed to operate the fishing boats, so supply can increase (right shift).

Next, let's take a look at the change in the **competitive environment:** If the number of competitors increases, the general supply will experience an increase. Therefore, a sudden increase from the environment will result in an increase in volume while the price remains the same (right shift). Another conceivable situation would be that many competitors have to close their business for reasons of insolvency, so that there are only a few competitors left. In this case, the supply is reduced (left shift).

What role do **taxes and subsidies** play in the supply situation? If the fishing company is subsidized, for example, it has more money available and can catch more fish and bring them to the customer on the market (right shift). If, however, the company has to pay higher taxes, this has the opposite effect (left shift).

What about certain **expectations**? If a boom in demand for fish is expected, because it is considered very healthy at the moment, for example, people will logically do everything they can to utilize their production and produce as much as possible (right shift). A poor expectation for the future, on the other hand, will result in a reduction in production volume (left shift).

Demand curve

Demand is the intention of demanders to purchase a product or service. The law of demand states that price determines the level of demand. Normally, a price reduction causes an increase in demand: if the price of a carton of milk has fallen by half, for example, people will consequently buy more milk. As with the supply function, here the demand function puts this context of price and quantity demanded into a mathematical formula. The demand curve is therefore a graphical representation of this function. Where the demand curve intersects the x-axis, there is **market saturation**, which is the quantity demanded at a price of zero. The **prohibitive price**, on the other hand, describes a price at which no one will buy the product and the quantity demanded will therefore be zero.

> **Important.** The sum of the demand quantities of all market participants is defined as the aggregated demanded quantity.
>
> Example: If 2 friends go shopping together and want to buy 2 packs of milk each, with no other customers in the store, the aggregate quantity demanded is equal to 4. Together with the supply curve, equilibrium price and market equilibrium can be determined.

Inverse demand function

The relationship between quantity demanded and price is inverse. The fact that the price is dependent on the quantity demanded is shown in the classic demand curve. For example, if 5 packs of milk are purchased, the price is 3 euros. However, one could also rephrase this: If the price is 3 euros, people are willing to buy 5 packs of milk. This two-way relationship is equivalent to a swap of the x and y axes - resulting in the inverse demand function.

Shift of the demand curve

The quantity demanded is not always dependent on price alone. In some cases, demand itself can increase or decrease, completely detached from price and only due to various external factors that result in a change in the market situation.

This is referred to as the parallel shift of the demand curve. An increase in the quantity demanded causes a parallel shift to the right.

There are different factors that can cause a shift in the demand function. These can be divided into 4 categories:

• Consumers change their tastes or **preferences.** For example, if it can be proven that the consumption of fish contributes to better health, the demand for fish will increase (right shift).

• Another influencing factor is the **number of consu-mers**. The steady population growth in China, for example, leads to an increase in aggregate market demand (rightward shift).

• The **price of other goods influences** demand. A distinction is made here between complements and substitutes. For muesli, for example, milk is a complementary good. If the demand for muesli increases, it is to be expected that the quantity of milk demanded will also increase (right shift). A substitute for milk can be soy milk, for example. If the relative price of this drops, customers are likely to buy more soy milk and save on cow's milk in return (left shift).

• Not to be neglected is the income of the customer. If income falls while the product price remains the same, the consumer will be able to afford less. Consequently, demand will fall (left shift).

From theory to practice

THE MOST IMPORTANT PRACTI-CAL TIPS FOR MORE REVENUE GENERATION FROM MARKETING

Marketing and sales. They are often mentioned in the same breath, which suggests a perfect match - just like coffee and cake. In practice, however, the relationship between the two is more reminiscent of water and oil.

For many different reasons, the perceptions of sales and marketing teams can go in very different directions. It is worth taking a look at the causes in order to be able to solve these problems. Terms should be defined on both sides and the placement of marketing and sales in the customer journey clearly determined.

Nothing should then stand in the way of harmonious collaboration. After all, both pursue the common goal of generating more leads (i.e., a qualified contact with a prospect) and sales.

In this chapter, we want to provide 5 suggestions to help all companies better align their marketing and sales efforts. They contain a mixture of philosophical and technical approaches that should lead to a better understanding of the processes.

Tip 1: Establish common definitions.
It is one of the biggest differences between marketing and sales and stems from divergent understandings of what is and is not an appropriate lead.

Marketing often looks too much at the quantity of leads and less at their quality, as they feel some pressure from sales management to bring forward as many leads as possible here . As a result, sales complains that the prospects provided do not meet the necessary requirements and are therefore of poor quality. This, in turn, leads to low close rates for the sales force. If, on the other hand, marketing and sales can clearly define together in advance what is meant by a qualified lead, many problems of this kind can be avoided.

A good way can be a sales and marketing meeting where relevant terms are brought to life in collaboration (e.g.: lead, qualified lead and highly qualified lead). But how do you arrive at these insights? To do this, first gather and convert typical characteristics of leads. Try creating checklists that can be tracked in a CRM system, for example. Each lead should meet a minimum set of qualifying elements to move to the next step in the sales cycle.

Tip 2: Use sales data.
Once agreement has been reached on defining a qualified lead, further effort is needed to improve lead quality in order to achieve satisfactory close potential. In a survey conducted by the B2B Technology Marketing Community, 61% of marketers cited poor lead quality as the primary obstacle to success. The obstacle is understandable. After all, customers today have much more choice and can draw from more sources of information than ever before.

This advantage can and should, of course, be leveraged by marketing and sales teams. So start with a healthy and clearly defined mix of demographic data (e.g., what occupations or functions do buyers from the target audience primarily perform) and behavioral data (e.g., which ad campaign or insert leads to more conversions) to incorporate into the lead evaluation process. By mapping sales closures from a particular campaign in a sales automation system, reports can reveal which targeting and marketing message is delivering the best-qualified leads. Linking other data sources and social media to lead records gives you a solid process for lead qualification. Both marketing and sales need to realize that quality often comes at a price - fewer leads in this context, which takes some courage. However, with accurate targeting, it's also easier and more efficient to realize the sales goals that have been set. In the end, it's a win-win situation: sales' pipeline is cleaned up and salespeople can focus on working the truly qualified leads.

Tip 3: Create integration between marketing and sales tools.

Logical - you would think. Unfortunately, however, the reality is that many companies continue to act in too much isolation when it comes to deploying and managing marketing and sales systems.

For example, people often simply buy lists of records and bombard them with emails. The responses are then quickly passed on to sales. Of course, this simple path can also lead to sales, but there is a better one: Using an integrated sales and marketing system, the lead generation path is much more sophisticated. Here, several software products can be used at the same time.

scoring and nurturing mechanisms (i.e., targeting prospects with relevant information at the right time), companies can automate the process of passing qualified leads to the sales department. This allows sales reps to invest all their energy in the leads most likely to close a sale.

Tip 4: Achieve best practices (i.e., proven or best practices) through optimal and intelligent workflows.

Qualified contacts can fall through the cracks even with an integrated marketing and sales automation system.

While a scoring method can automatically trigger the routing of leads to sales, it is possible for leads to be mismeasured by sales tools or to receive inadequate treatment on the part of sales reps. If "hot" contacts are not to cool, lead status must be properly tracked and controls must be in place. This is the only way to ensure timely follow-up by sales reps and to stay ahead of the competition.

A modern workflow in the process of forwarding and managing new contacts within a CRM system can already remedy this situation. For example, this workflow can monitor various actions - or failure to act -

when forwarded to a specific sales representative, and hand them off to a less busy colleague if not handled within a specific time period. This method increases the potential for converting prospects to buyers and ensures a positive and seamless buying experience for the acquired customer.

Tip 5: Gain a holistic view of your customers.
The bad news is, CRM and marketing systems can't record all customer behaviors. The good news is that there is a whole wealth of customer data in other systems that can be used to improve business performance. For example, enterprise resource planning (ERP) and billing systems contain information about transactions that can be evaluated and integrated with marketing and sales data.

This makes it much easier to target customers with really high potential. Data from social media channels also often provides further insights into the preferences and behaviors of the target group. In any case, multiple internal and external sources should be reviewed. This can ensure that contact data is error-free, which further optimizes the effectiveness of advertising campaigns.

Summary
Today's business world is diverse and demanding. This has changed the guidelines in marketing. Prospects do more research and information before contacting sales. Creating seamless systems, taking an unconditional customer view, and making the most of the wealth of data available about customers or those who are about to become customers can promote harmonious collaboration between marketing and sales. The end result is higher quality customer contacts and a productive in-house handoff with higher close rates. Today, we are in the fortunate position that advanced, cost-effective technologies already exist to support this effort. Ultimately, every company has the power to build a stable bridge between marketing and sales by choosing flexible software.

AND NOW YOU: 10 STEPS TO YOUR MARKETING PLAN

Marketing can sometimes be a maze. There are so many ways and means to achieve success.

However, this diversity can also easily overwhelm you, especially if you are still at the beginning. To conclude this guide, we would therefore like to make it a little easier for you to get started in practice and provide you with 10 simple steps for creating a practical marketing plan.

Step 1: Determine your target audience and develop an understanding of their problem.

The most important basis for successful product marketing is precise knowledge of the target group, knowledge of wishes, problems or challenges. Narrowing down these people as precisely as possible enables a targeted approach.

Step 2: Get to the bottom of your USP.

Why should your target group choose your product over the competition's? What is your why? What conviction does your company have and what does it stand for?

More and more prospects these days are finding out about an organization's message and values and evaluating whether they match their own. So your company needs a clear motivation why a well-informed prospect should choose your good. In any case, a clear answer should be found here. This clear answer is called a USP (Unique Selling Proposition) in the brand ting environment and refers to a unique selling proposition, i.e., something that only your company can offer or that distinguishes your offerings.

Step 3: Develop customer enthusiasm.
This step is to find a precise definition for the customer's benefit. How exactly do you build your offering to evoke excitement in your customers and ideally even exceed their expectations? Here are some principles for a great customer experience:

- Customer satisfaction should not be a coincidence, but precisely planned.
- Put positive social components in place.
- Give your customers a sense of control.

Step 4: Formulate promise and guarantee.
This is about presenting the previously determined things to the customer. Everything that was previously noted and decided must now be "packaged" in an appealing and convincing way so that your customers can develop trust.

Step 5: Create an irresistible offer to get started.
The implementation of the first 4 steps now provides you with an important basis for your marketing activities. Step 5 should lower the inhibition threshold for your customers to enter into an initial business relationship with your company.

The aim is therefore to convince prospective customers of a specific, enticing offer. Acquiring new customers usually swallows up the largest share of the marketing budget, which is justified if a functioning marketing concept is in place.

Step 6: Putting content into the right words.
Now you've come this far, you've thought about what your vision and USPs are, what you want to promise your customers, and what entry-level offering sounds particularly compelling.

All of this must now be translated into good, clearly formulated advertising texts, because nothing makes it more difficult for your customers to decide in favor of your offer than boring texts that are difficult to understand - no matter how good the offer itself may be. So, however you want to market your pro ducts, the texts you use will make the difference between success and failure.

Step 7: Establish a sequence in the marketing process.
This is where it is defined how and where the relevant target group can best be addressed and converted step by step from first contact to profitable regular custo-mers. Every customer goes through different stages

before buying a product, which may vary somewhat depending on the industry.

The technical term in marketing is funnel. You can imagine a prospect being led into the funnel from above and coming out at the bottom as a customer. Unfortunately, in reality, not all of the people introduced at the top come out at the bottom as actual customers. This is because the so-called funnel has holes through which potential prospects can fall out at any stage. The primary goal must therefore be to plug these holes as best as possible and at the same time to lead as many new prospects as possible into the funnel at the top.

Step 8: Define channels for customer engagement.

In step 7, the respective stages of the marketing process were defined. Step 8 should now clarify which options potential buyers can use to move from one stage to the next. Here, you need to carefully consider which sales channels work best, where the target group is well represented, and which channels fit well with your company and product offerings. For example, rollators for seniors should not be advertised on the video portal TikTok, which is popular with teenagers. Focus on the selected channels instead of trying as many as possible.

Step 9: Develop number sense.
Now, before applying what you have learned, it is still of immense importance to understand your numbers accurately.

Many people deal intensively with marketing, but lose focus on the numbers. Understanding marketing and calculating its success requires a meaningful calculation. Only if you know your numbers can you judge whether your marketing activities make sense or whether your numbers need to be improved. In short: Successful marketing absolutely requires an understanding of numbers.

Step 10: Find strong partners.
It's time to say congratulations. At this point, you have laid the foundation for entering into partnerships in marketing, because good collaborations are crucial to your success. In many industries, they are part of the norm and mean an advantage for all parties involved. This is especially the case when several companies address the same target group and offer similar products.

Conclusion: This is your marketing plan

As you can see, it can also be easy to set up a business-ready marketing strategy. It is not necessary to read thick textbooks or have a degree. Common sense can create so much, especially considering that the steps of a marketing concept are very similar in all industries.

www.ingramcontent.com/pod-product-compliance
Lightning Source LLC
Chambersburg PA
CBHW031452130726
47989CB00003B/1349